THE LIFE AND DEATH OF DINOSAURS

(Original French title: *Vie et Mort des Dinosaures*)

by

Pascale Chenel

Illustrated by Bernard Girodroux

Translated from the French by

Albert V. Carozzi and Marguerite Carozzi

BARRON'S

New York • London • Toronto • Sydney

First English language edition published in 1987 by
Barron's Educational Series, Inc.

© 1986 Hachette S.A., 79, boulevard Saint-Germain, 75006 Paris

The title of the French edition is *Vie et Mort des Dinosaures.*

All inquiries should be addressed to:
Barron's Educational Series, Inc.
250 Wireless Boulevard
Hauppauge, New York 11788

International Standard Book No. 0-8120-3840-1
Library of Congress Catalog Card No. 87-24105

Library of Congress Cataloging-in-Publication Data

Chenel, Pascale.
  The life and death of dinosaurs.
  (Barron's Focus on Science)
  Translation of: Vie et mort des dinosaures.
  Includes index.
  Summary: Focuses on what the study of fossil remains
has revealed about the nature, life, and death of the
dinosaurs.
  1. Dinosaurs—Juvenile literature. [1. Dinosaurs.
2. Paleontology] I. Girodroux, Bernard, ill.
II. Title.
QE862.D5C4913   1987   567.9'1   87-24105
ISBN 0-8120-3840-1

PRINTED IN ITALY
890 9912 98765432

Contents

THE GEOLOGIC TIME SCALE

ERA	PERIOD	BEGAN: (millions of years before present)	CLIMATE
CENOZOIC	QUATERNARY	1.8	Rather cool with glaciations
	TERTIARY	5	Cooling
		25	Warm
		40	Warm
		55	Rather warm in the northern hemisphere
		65	Increasingly colder toward the poles
MESOZOIC	CRETACEOUS	135	Warm with rainy seasons
	JURASSIC	200	Warm and increasingly humid
	TRIASSIC	225	Warm and dry; deserts
PALEOZOIC	PERMIAN	280	Similar to that of Carboniferous
	CARBONIFEROUS	300	Warm and very humid in the northern hemisphere; glacial in the southern hemisphere
	DEVONIAN	395	Warm and often dry
	SILURIAN	440	Warmer
	ORDOVICIAN	500	Becoming warmer
	CAMBRIAN	600	At first cold, then becoming average
	PRECAMBRIAN	4600	Atmosphere low in oxygen; cold with warmer periods

ANIMAL LIFE	PLANT LIFE
Java man and Peking man	Development of arctic flora
Australopithecus in Africa at the end of this epoch	Development of flora in temperate zones
Numerous anthropoids; grazing mammals	Appearance of herbaceous plants
First anthropoids	Increase of flowering plants
Strange herbivorous mammals; first horses and elephants	Flowering trees predominate
Mammals evolve and take the place of reptiles	Development of flowering plants; decrease of Cycadeoidess
At the end of this period, extinction of dinosaurs, ammonites, and other marine life	Appearance of flowering plants
Ammonites, new corals, and sea urchins; dinosaurs; flying reptiles and first birds; small mammals	Giant ferns; Cycadeoidess and Ginkgoales
Appearance of dinosaurs and marine reptiles; end of mammallike reptiles; first mammals	Predominance of conifers; appearance of Cycadeoidess and of Bennettitales
Development of reptiles; extinction of trilobites	Development of conifers
Development of amphibians leading to reptiles; insects	Giant lycopods, ferns, horsetails; first conifers
Age of fish; appearance of amphibians	Spread of terrestrial plants: ferns
Jawless and armored fish; first fish with jaws	Algae; first terrestrial plants: Psilopsida
Graptolites, trilobites, corals, brachiopods, first vertebrates	Algae and perhaps primitive mosses and lichens
Appearance of the first groups of invertebrates (trilobites)	Lime-secreting algae
Traces of animal life in rocks less than 1 billion years old	Algae, bacteria

Spotlight on the Dinosaurs

Are you ready for an extraordinary trip? Close your eyes. Step into your time-exploring machine and travel 225 million years into the past. You are now in the Triassic (the first period of the Mesozoic). The climate is warm and dry and varies little from one area to another. Most of the earth's surface is covered by vast oceans, but there is one continent, Pangaea, which formed during the last period of the Paleozoic (Permian). Animals are able to occupy all parts of the world.

This single continent did not last very long on the geologic time scale: 25 million years. At the beginning of the Jurassic, the second period of the Mesozoic, it started to break up into two parts: Laurasia (today's North America, Europe, and Asia) and Gondwana (today's South America, Africa, India, and Antarctica). A narrow and deep seaway called Tethys separated the two new continents. The new continents were, however, still connected to each other at one place through which land animals could migrate. Shallower seas covered certain places of Laurasia (see map: The world during the Cretaceous). This was very important because these large areas of water brought to Laurasia a warmer and more humid climate. At the beginning of the Cretaceous, the third and last period of the Mesozoic, 135 million years before the present, the Tethyan seaway enlarged and the northern and southern continents completely separated. Around the same time a shallow sea parted most of what is now Africa from the rest of Gondwana.

In the middle of the Cretaceous, the sea further invaded the continents. South America, Antarctica, and Australia were soon parted from the Indian continent. Shallow seas also split North America into two parts.

View at the beginning of the Cretaceous: *This is, of course, a re-creation by an illustrator. In the foreground, an Iguanodon feeds on leaves and a Hypsilophodon steals some eggs, while in the background, a carnivorous Megalosaurus lies in wait for the two.*

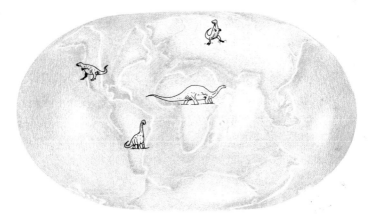

The world during the Triassic: *The world had a completely different aspect 200 million years ago, than it does today. All the continents were united into a supercontinent, called Pangaea. This was at the end of the Paleozoic and allowed fauna and flora to spread over all the continents. Thus, at the end of the Triassic, dinosaurs—which had just appeared—occupied every part of the world.*

The world during the Cretaceous: *At the end of the Triassic and the beginning of the Jurassic, the supercontinent started to break up. During the Cretaceous, 100 million years ago, the northern continents separated from the southern continents. North and South America parted from Europe, Africa, and Antarctica. A shallow sea divided North America into two continents. Another sea, the Tethys, separated Africa from Eurasia.*

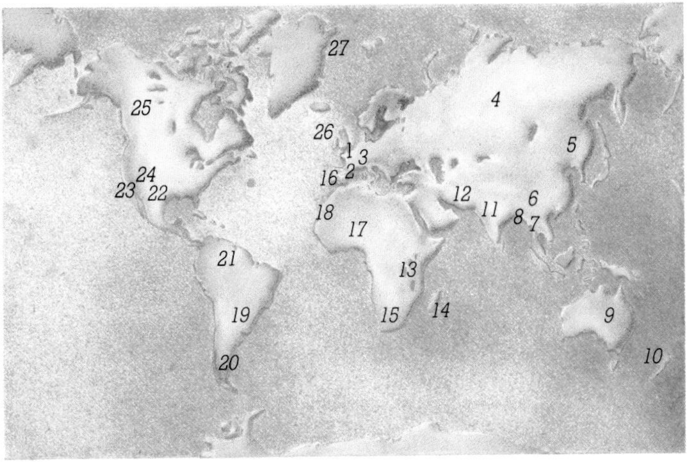

Main occurrences of fossil dinosaurs in the world

1 Normandy (France)

2 Provence (France)

3 Germany

4 Gobi Desert (Mongolia)

5 Manchuria (northeast China)

6 Yunnan and Szechwan (China)

7 Muang Phalane (Laos)

8 Phu Wiang (Thialand)

9 Queensland (Australia)

10 New Zealand

11 Dekkan (India)

12 Kerman (Iran)

13 Tendaguru (Tanzania)

14 Madagascar

15 Lesotho (South Africa)

16 Spain

17 Gadoufaoua (Niger)

18 Morocco

19 Bauru (Brazil)

20 Patagonia (Argentina)

21 Venezuela

22 New Mexico (United States)

23 Colorado (United States)

24 Wyoming (United States)

25 Alberta (Canada)

26 London Basin (Great Britain)

27 Spitsbergen (Norway)

During the Mesozoic, the continents acquired their distinctive characteristics. At the beginning of the Triassic, a hot and dry climate prevailed. During the Jurassic and the Cretaceous, as the inland seas became larger, the climate in many areas became more humid while remaining hot. Seasons hardly existed. Mountain chains including the Andes and the Rocky Mountains, were formed. They created a barrier against rain-producing clouds, causing rain to fall on one slope of the mountain while the other side remained dry. The climate influenced vegetation, which proliferated and became luxurious and more varied (as in present tropical countries).

Animals also adapted and diversified according to the area where they lived. Reptiles dominated the earth: dinosaurs on land, pterosaurs in the air, and ichthyosaurs, plesiosaurs, and turtles in the sea. The first birds appeared during the Late Jurassic (140 million years ago). Mammals existed already but merely survived in the shadow of the dinosaurs. Insects existed in profusion.

Plants evolved on land. Ferns, which had existed since the Devonian (fourth period of the Paleozoic, almost 400 million years ago) became abundant. Conifers (pine trees and fir trees) had continued to evolve since the Carboniferous (fifth period of the Paleozoic, about 340 million years ago). Cycads (palmlike trees) appeared during the Triassic.

Flowering plants made their debut during the Cretaceous and spread rapidly over the entire earth; some were real trees in terms of height; others, such as duckweeds, measured only a few millimeters. The flowers themselves varied greatly. There is not much difference between present-day plants and those that lived 80 million years ago.

The Reign of the Dinosaurs

When the first dinosaurs appeared in the Late Triassic, reptiles had already conquered the earth 100 million years earlier.

Our knowledge of dinosaurs is extensive but has many gaps: we know only

Saurischians and Ornithischians

*Saurischian dinosaurs differ from ornithischians
mainly by the shape of the pelvis. Ornithischians
have a birdlike pelvis, whereas saurischians have a
lizardlike pelvis.*
Saurischians are divided into two suborders:
*Sauropods, herbivorous quadrupeds (such as
Brachiosaurus and Diplodocus) and*
*Theropods, carnivorous bipeds subdivided into
Coelurosaurs, the smaller ones
Carnosaurs, the larger ones (for example,
Tyrannosaurus)*
*All ornithischians are herbivorous. They are sub-
divided into several suborders:*
*Stegosaurs and their relatives
Ankylosaurs (quadrupeds)
Ceratopians (quadrupeds)
Pachycephalosaurs (bipeds)*

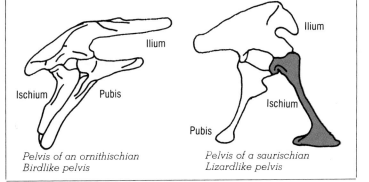

*Pelvis of an ornithischian
Birdlike pelvis*

*Pelvis of a saurischian
Lizardlike pelvis*

RECONSTRUCTION OF A JURASSIC LANDSCAPE

The warm and humid tropical climate of this period was perfectly suited to dinosaurs. Vegetation was luxurious, with predominant ferns and conifers. Flowers did not yet exist: they appeared at the end of the Cretaceous.

1. Arborescent ferns.

2. Cycads. These plants appeared in the Triassic and flourished during the Jurassic and the Cretaceous. Some of them still live today.

3. Ferns.

4. Calamites were giant horsetails, a plant still living today but of much smaller size.

5. Conifers.

6. Compsognathus was a saurischian dinosaur at the end of the Jurassic. It is

one of the smallest known dinosaurs: adults barely reach 1 meter (3 feet) in height.

7. Psaronius was an arborescent fern.

8. Archaeopteryx appeared in the Jurassic. It was the first known bird, although unable to really fly. It still resembled a reptile. As tall as a pigeon, it had claws on the wings, teeth in the beak, and a long tail. It must have caught its prey on the ground after gliding. Its descendants, the true birds, began to proliferate at the end of the Cretaceous.

9. The gingko thrived during the Jurassic. Its fan-shaped leaves gave it the aspect of a flowering tree. However, real flowers appeared only at the end of the Cretaceous. An ornamental species of Chinese origin that still embellishes botanical gardens, the gingko was limited to China until two centures ago. Travelers imported it to Europe and also to North America, where it did very well.

what their skeletons reveal, the climatic conditions under which they lived, and their contemporary fauna and flora.

Dinosaurs are divided into two major orders: saurischians and ornithischians, which differ by the structure of the jaw and pelvis. Saurischians had a lizard-like pelvis and ornithischians had a birdlike pelvis.

All ornithischians and most saurischians were herbivorous. In the saurischians, only theropods, a suborder including coelurosaurs and carnosaurs, were carnivorous. These two major orders do not seem to have had a common ancestor. They are believed to have evolved independently.

Some 600 different species of dinosaurs have been found, and studies of dinosaur localities are far from completion. Others will certainly be found.

Whether bipeds or quadrupeds, herbivores or carnivores, dinosaurs gradually invaded the earth. Beginning in the Triassic, they evolved into numerous and diversified lineages. Their maximum development was in the Jurassic.

As always in the animal kingdom, herbivores largely predominated over carnivores. Herbivores tended to live in herds, whereas carnivores were often solitary hunters.

As all reptiles, dinosaurs laid eggs. In 1922, a nest of eggs of *Protoceratops* (a Cretaceous dinosaur) was found dug into the sand of the Gobi Desert in Mongolia. A single nest contained eighteen eggs arranged in a circle. It is assumed that the female was watching its eggs or laying them when attacked and killed by a small biped dinosaur that wanted to prey on them. Indeed, both skeletons were found interlocked, mute evidence of the fight to the death between a mother and an egg snatcher.

Strange Shapes

Coelophysis (a coelurosaur, hence a carnivore), one of the oldest known dinosaurs, was a biped animal, 2.5 meters (8 feet) long. Slender and fast, it ran on its hindlegs and used its forelegs to catch its prey.

Plateosaurus (saurischian) and **Heterodontosaurus** (ornithischian), both herbivorous, were very different from each other.

Egg Laying and Nests of Dinosaurs

Dinosaur eggs were found arranged in a circle. It is assumed that the female moved in a clockwise direction as she laid her eggs one by one.

Cross-section of other egg nests of dinosaurs. These nests seem to indicate that females used distinct and regular places for laying eggs: the blue eggs at the bottom represent a first laying, the pink eggs a second.

A herd of Diplodocus:
As did most herbivorous dinosaurs, they moved about in groups.

Whereas the first one, bulky and heavy, moved slowly on its four legs and was an easy prey for carnivores, the second, barely taller than a turkey, was very fast and capable of avoiding danger.

These three dinosaurs lived during the Triassic. Later, during the Jurassic and the Cretaceous, these large reptiles multiplied and displayed more and more extravagant shapes.

Sauropods must have spent most of their time searching for food because the head was extremely small compared to the huge size of the body. The jaws did not allow them to swallow much food at one time. These gigantic animals, in spite of their size, must have been the ideal prey for large carnosaurs, such as *Allosaurus* (Jurassic) and *Tyrannosaurus* (Cretaceous).

Brachiosaurus, a famous sauropod of the Jurassic, was more than 25 meters (82 feet) long, weighed almost 80 tons, and raised its head 13 meters (42 feet) high—the height of a five-story building — in order to

16

Cold-blooded Animals?

Reptiles are cold-blooded animals that lose or gain heat through the skin. Dinosaurs have long been thought to have been cold-blooded—like other reptiles. Cold-bloodedness may have led to problems for the dinosaurs, however. The larger an animal, the smaller is the surface of its skin compared with its volume, and therefore its adaptation to variations in temperature becomes increasingly slow as size increases. We know that some dinosaurs were very large. This leads to the assumption that they were not capable of adapting quickly to great changes in temperature. The tropical climate at the beginning of the Mesozoic would have presented no problem for most of them, but the cooling that occurred at the end of that era might have been lethal to them. In recent years, however, some scientists have postulated that dinosaurs may have been warm-blooded.

eat the tender leaves on the treetops. It lived in herds, as did its relative *Diplodocus*—only 25 meters (80 feet) long—whose footprints were found in the soft mud at the edge of swamps. These tracks indicate that it moved together with forty other *Diplodocus*, adults surrounding and protecting the young in the middle of the herd.

Stegosaurs lived during the Jurassic. These peaceful ornithischians fed on the abundant vegetation on the ground. They were about 7 meters (22 feet) tall with hindlegs twice as long as forelegs. They could not run fast when chased by carnivores, but their tails bristled with long and very dangerous bony spikes. Furthermore, the back and neck were protected by a row of verticular triangular bony plates. A real fortress! The only weakness of the armor was the flanks.

Stegosaurs disappeared at the end of the Jurassic and were replaced during the Cretaceous by ankylosaurs, slightly smaller but even better protected. *Ankylosaurus*, standing on short and stubby legs, had a large and flattened body that carried on the back bony plates full of spikes and a club at the end of the tail! For protection, there was nothing better. Nevertheless, it was the prey of the terrible *Tyrannosaurus*. It was 14 meters (45 feet) long, the most horrible carnivore the earth ever witnessed. Biped, it stood 5 meters (17 feet) above the ground. Its head was a nightmare: 1.4 meters (4.5 feet) long carrying teeth 20 centimeters (8 inches) in size.

Iguanodons were ornithopods of the early Cretaceous. These herbivores had several rows of side teeth that, when abraded, were replaced by new ones. The *iguanodon* was a biped more than 9 meters (30 feet) long. The tail counterbalanced the heavy and muscular body. The rather small forelegs had a bony thumb shaped into a sharp spike that helped in defense, but they could also run away rather fast from carnivores. They lived in herds. The fossil remains of about twenty *iguanodons* were found in Belgium buried under a landslide.

Hadrosaurs were ornithopods living in the Late Cretaceous. Some were disovered as mummies with perfectly preserved skin. Very tall, 9 to 12 meters (30 to 40 feet) long, they were "duck-billed"; that is, the skull and the lower jaw formed a large horny beak. Inside, almost a thousand closely spaced teeth could finely grind food. Their head carried a "crest" of uncertain use. Perhaps it improved their sense of smell or increased the intensity of their shrieks.

Ceratopsians resembled rhinoceroses and lived during the Late Cretaceous. For instance, *Triceratops* had two horns (1 meter, or 3 feet, long) above the eyes and another on top of the snout. It had a bony shield that protected the nape, neck, and shoulders. It was a real beast, 7 meters (23 feet) long, which could even charge ferocious carnosaurs.

Pachycephalosaurus, *a dinosaur of the end of the Cretaceous. Its skull was thickened in the rear and above the eyes by bony spikes and bulges. It must have used this "helmet" to fight in a way similar to modern deer and rams. However, some scientists think that this "helmet" served to regulate temperature.*

A Great Diversity

Dinosaurs were without any doubt the most diversified reptiles. Some were as small as a chicken; others reached 30 meters (100 feet) in length. This great variation in size and shape of the body was an effect of the various environments to which they had to adapt.

SAURISCHIANS

Plateosaurus
Prosauropod – 8 meters (25 feet)

Tyrannosaurus
Carnosaur – 14 meters (45 feet)

Diplodocus
Sauropod – 25 meters (80 feet)

Coelophysis
Coelophysis – 2.5 meters (8 feet)

ORNITHISCHIANS

Ankylosaurus
Ankylosaur – 9 meters (29 feet)

Triceratops
Ceratopsian – 7 meters (23 feet)

Hadrosaurus
Ornithopod – 9 meters (30 feet)

Iguanodon
Ornithopod – 9 meters (30 feet)

Stegosaurus
Stegosaur – 7 meters (22 feet)

Pachycephalosaurus carried on the top of its head a bony mass more than 25 centimeters (10 inches) thick. Its use has not yet been determined. Was it used when fighting an enemy? Was it used for thermal regulation?

By means of their fossilized bones, dinosaur skeletons have been reconstructed. This fascinating work started in the nineteenth century and is far from complete. How could animals that lived 200 million years ago be reconstructed?

Tyrannosaurus, *a dinosaur at the end of the Cretaceous*

These Are Not Dinosaurs

Dinosaurs lived only on land. At the same time, two other groups of reptiles lived in the sea: ichthyosaurs and plesiosaurs. Another reptile, Pterosaurus, *reaching up to 15 meters (50 feet) in wingspan, glided in the air. Finally,* Dimetrodon *was a mammallike reptile, an ancestor of mammals.*

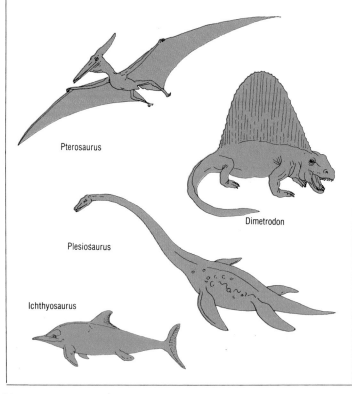

Pterosaurus

Dimetrodon

Plesiosaurus

Ichthyosaurus

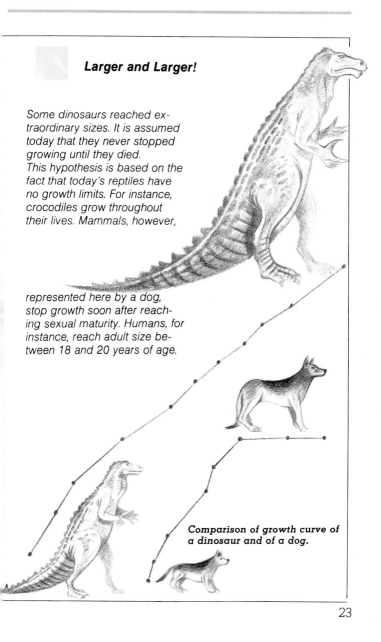

Larger and Larger!

Some dinosaurs reached extraordinary sizes. It is assumed today that they never stopped growing until they died.
This hypothesis is based on the fact that today's reptiles have no growth limits. For instance, crocodiles grow throughout their lives. Mammals, however,

represented here by a dog, stop growth soon after reaching sexual maturity. Humans, for instance, reach adult size between 18 and 20 years of age.

Comparison of growth curve of a dinosaur and of a dog.

On the Tracks of the Dinosaurs

You may have found in the field some strange "stones" shaped like shells. These are probably fossils of animals that lived some tens of millions years ago. Since antiquity, humans have wondered about the significance of these strange stones. It seems that some prehistoric humans even collected them! Many explanations of their formation have been given. For instance, Empedocles, a Greek philosopher of the fifth century B.C., believed that nature first created imperfect shapes, which were later abandoned. Pliny the Elder, the Roman naturalist and writer of the first century A.D., declared that fossil shark teeth were petrified tongues fallen from the sky during lunar eclipses. Today, it is known that since the beginning, nature has undergone perpetual change and that some animal and plant species once existed and then vanished. Geologists are able to date rock layers and fossils included in these rocks. Likewise, the study of dinosaur bones allows us to infer the size, shape, and ways of living of the dinosaurs.

What happens after the death of an animal? If it dies in a forest, all of it rapidly disappears. Carnivores devour its corpse, then ants and bacteria clean up the scraps. The bones are scattered and eventually become unrecognizable. In a desert, a dead animal may be mummified or differences in temperature between day and night may be so great that bones break up and are slowly reduced to powder.

In contrast, if the animal is rapidly buried in mud or sand, its hard parts may be preserved. When a swamp dries up, for instance, it surrounds the bones with a matrix of solid mud and preserves them.

Where Are Fossils Found?

There are five particular environments that are favorable for fossilization.

Swamps: It may happen that terrestrial animals, carried away by storms, drown or sink into swamps. Over millions of years, the sediments in the swamps harden and preserve the dead animals almost intact.

Lakes: Dead animal bodies, when transported by a river to a lake, are deposited on the bottom, where they are covered by a layer of clay that protects them. Their skeletons are

Fossil dinosaur footprint:
This is believed to be a ornithopod because of the membrane that connects the fingers: it had webbed feet.

often not entirely preserved, however, because they generally break apart in the river currents. However, when animals sank into mud bordering a lake, entire skeletons may be found.

Rivers: Fossils may be preserved in the coarse sand in rivers when animals are carried away by floods. After the waters become calm, the animals sink to the bottom and are buried in mud or sand that was stirred up during the flood. In general, there, too, one finds fossils of disarticulated skeletons because of their transportation by water.

Caves: Rainwater often carries red clay underground into caves or caverns. If an animal falls into a cave, it may be covered by this clay and be fossilized.

The Sea: Numerous small marine animals were fossilized in the calm waters of some bays. Sometimes one finds unusual fossil sites where there are entire marine fish and reptiles, including the scales and fins of the former and entire

Fossil tracks of dinosaurs: *tracks of two different dinosaurs can be noticed here: the first (large tracks) coming out from the water (1) and the other*

1

Shore

limbs and remains of skin of the latter. The causes are the fine nature of the mud and its extremely slow hardening.

Thus buried over millions and millions of years, bones and shells undergo changes as the sediment around them hardens. This is how fossils are formed. Sometimes, one even finds the imprints of skin, feathers, hair, or eggs. Even plants can be fossilized.

An extraordinary case of fossilization occurred in the frozen soils of Siberia. A herd of mammoths was buried there, and when the animals were discovered, they looked as if they had died the day before. They had been frozen stiff before fossilization.

One sometimes finds fossilized insects in amber. Amber itself is the fossil resin of pines. Before fossilization of this resin, insects became glued to it. They can be seen today, still complete, and all the details of their bodies can be admired: legs, wings with delicate veins, and so on. Fossils are not only remains of animals and

(smaller tracks) show that the animal went several times to drink along the shore (2). These tracks were discovered in Lesotho, Southern Africa.

2

Traces left by the water

27

plants, however. They may also be evidence of their lives: footprints, traces of fighting...

Shipping of Fossils

To extract a skeleton or part of a skeleton from a rock formation requires much time, work, and patience. At first, the rock must be gradually chipped off and disaggregated and the debris brushed away until the bones are exposed without having been dis-placed. This is necessary so that paleontologists may know exactly how the bones were arranged. Then, photographs are taken. Finally, the bones are removed and brought to the laboratory, which is also not an easy task because bones crumble easily. When the first dinosaurs were discovered in the United States (in the 1870s), fossils were transported over open country and rough roads by four-wheeled wagons—and they

A paleontologist at work: *This paleontologist, using his pickax, attempts to extract a dinosaur jaw from the rock.*

often arrived in crumbs. One day, the American paleontologist Edward D. Cope had an excellent idea. At that time, the basic staple for expeditions was rice. Cope hated it. He had the idea to cook the rice until it formed a thick paste. Then he soaked bands of jute (a coarse plant material) in it and then used them to wrap the fossils. After hardening, this mixture efficiently protected its valuable contents. This basic technique was continued, but rice was replaced by plaster.

When large bones are extracted, the upper part is exposed and then covered by wet paper and bands of cloth soaked in plaster. Thereafter, the rock that encloses the lower part of the bone is chiseled out. The fossil is turned over and separated completely from the rock, and it is then covered with plaster. Finally, the bone is put in a well-padded box and sent to the laboratory.

Dinosaurs of North America

Beginning in the 1870s, some of the most exciting discoveries of dinosaur remains have been made in North America. Aside from some prosauropod fossils found in the Connecticut Valley, major deposits have been found in New Mexico, at Como Bluff in southern Wyoming, near Morrison, Colorado, at Hell Creek, Montana, and at the site of the present-day Dinosaur National Monument near Jensen, Utah. At the latter site, some 845 square kilometers (325 square miles) in area, visitors can view many of the steps in the recovery of dinosaur bones and see fossils that are still embedded in the rocks where they have been for tens of millions of years.

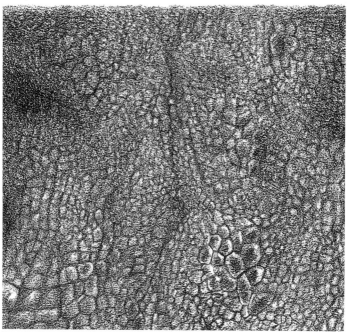

Fossil skin of a Hadrosaur. *This skin is so well preserved that all details are visible. It is assumed that the larger plates were of a different color from the rest.*

Since the 1960s, plaster has sometimes been replaced by polystyrene.

The Age of Fossils?

Once fossils are found, how does one determine the period when these animals lived?

At the beginning of the nineteenth century some people still believed that the earth was only 6000 years old. According to calculations based on the Scriptures, Archbishop James Ussher of Ireland wrote that the earth was created in the year 4004 before Christ.

The study by geologists of the superposition of rock layers soon allowed them to establish that the earth was much older.

Today, the age of fossils and rocks is established

by means of radiometric dating.

Every living being, every element of matter, contains radioactive particles that decay very slowly during a span of time that can be dated with precision. The older the fossil is, the fewer radioactive particles it contains, and different substances and techniques must be used to date fossils and rocks of different ages.

For instance, carbon 14 is used to date fossils that are 1000 to 70,000 years old; potassium 40 is used for those that are older than 100,000 years; rubidium 87 dates fossils that are older than 10 million years; and thorium 232 dates those that are older than 50 million years.

Fossils are very abundant, although four-fifths of the earth is covered by

The First Discovery of a Dinosaur

This happened in southern England, in the spring of 1822. While the physician Gideon Mantell visited a patient, his wife, Mary Ann Woodhouse Mantell, went for a walk in the countryside. She discovered on a rock several teeth of an unknown fossil animal. An enthusiastic amateur paleontologist, her husband continued her diggings and found the bones of a fabulous animal, which he named Iguanodon because of its resemblance to the American lizard, the iguana.

Mary Ann Mantell

oceans, leaving only a relatively small area to find traces of fossil animals and plants. Those found represent a very small number of those still buried. Every year discoveries of new forms of life, now extinct, are made.

Fabulous Discoveries

Starting in 1922, Roy Chapman Andrews, naturalist, explorer, and curator at the American Museum of Natural History in New York City, undertook several expeditions to the Gobi Desert in Mongolia. The unusual character of this desert is that it was never covered by the sea. Andrews thought the remains of terrestrial animals were likely to be found there. The expedition included twenty-six men in cars and a caravan of camels for the transportation of food and gasoline. Andrews was certain he would discover the remains of mammals that lived in the Cretaceous, between 65 and 135 million years ago.

Instead of mammals, they found an extraordinary fossil site of dinosaurs: the first to be excavated in Asia, north of the Hima-

layas. There were giant carnivores, duckbilled herbivores, and also the perfectly preserved skull of a dinosaur ancestor of *Triceratops*. It was called *Protoceratops andrewsi* in honor of the chief of the expedition. The expedition made another remarkable discovery: dinosaur eggs in large number. After 3 years, the Americans had gathered a unique collection of seventy-five skulls and twelve complete skeletons of *Protoceratops* from young to adults.

One Hundred and Twenty Tons of Bones

Later, in 1946, the Soviets explored the fabulous desert, too. Under the leadership of I. A. Efremov, they discovered another fossil site of dinosaurs, in which were several complete skeletons of the biped carnivorous *Tarbosaurus* (close relative of *Tyrannosaurus*). All together, 120 tons of bones were transported to Moscow.

From 1964 to 1971, a Polish group joined the Mongolians and made several expeditions. They carried 20 tons of supplies, a six-wheeled truck able to drive in sand dunes, and tents made especially for the desert. Further extraordinary discoveries were made during 7 years of work and research in the sand and rocks of the Gobi Desert.

Searching for dinosaurs again proved to be a success: scientists not only found another *Tarbosaurus* but in 1971 made a sensational discovery: a *Protoceratops* in a death grip in the claws of the small carnivore *Velociraptor*. For the first time, one could "see" a battle between two dinosaurs! They also found an ankylosaur, which they named *Saichana* from the Mongolian word *saichan*, which means "beautiful".

If You Want to Find Fossils

To discover fossils, you must search in cliffs, road ditches, and railroad cuts—everywhere rocks are exposed. There are more chances of finding something in sedimentary rocks consisting of very fine particles that were deposited a long time ago on the bottom of seas or lakes (clays, argillaceous shales, and limestones). On a geologic map, such sites are easily located.

It is better to choose a special hammer for geologists, a cold chisel (flat), or a pointed burin. Don't forget a helmet when climbing a cliff, for protection against possible rockfalls.

Once the fossil is extracted, clean it with a toothbrush or a toothpick. It must be labeled with care without forgetting to write down the place it was found.

If you find a fossil that looks important, you should not try to extract it, but should contact the nearest natural history museum.

How to Reconstruct a Dinosaur

Paleontologists have only fossils for information about the appearance of extinct animals. In fact, when discovered skeletons are too incomplete, the missing parts are inferred by comparison with other known animals.

For the first reconstruction of Iguanodon, the result was somewhat strange. In 1834, Gideon Mantell had in his possession several teeth and bones found by his wife at the same place. These fossil bones belonged to an animal much larger than those already known. Mantell therefore imagined the animal whose bones he had. He named it Iguanodon because its teeth resembled those of an iguana. Having no skeleton for comparison, he erred in his sketch (see below); he put the bony claw of the thumb on the head of the animal and thought that it was a quadruped whereas it was a biped instead.

Today, more scientific techniques are used in particular since our knowledge of dinosaurs has greatly increased.

From tibia to dinosaur. *With a hammer, chisel, and a brush, a paleontologist has disengaged the tibia of a dinosaur.*

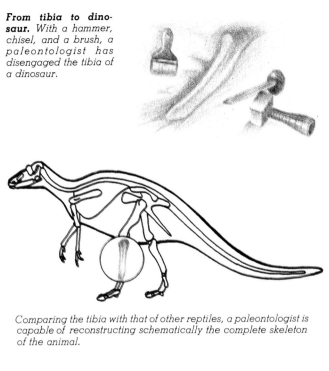

Comparing the tibia with that of other reptiles, a paleontologist is capable of reconstructing schematically the complete skeleton of the animal.

After the skeleton is constructed, it must be "clothed" with muscle. The imprints of muscle attachments and comparison with other animals allow reconstruction of the muscular system.

Learning from Footprints

Fossil footprints reveal the shape of the foot, the number of toes of a dinosaur, and whether it was a biped or a quadruped. According to the dimensions of footprints and their relation to the dimensions of the whole skeleton, it is possible to infer the size and even the stride of a dinosaur.

With measurements of the stride and calculation of the height above the ground of the pelvis and shoulder, it is then possible to calculate the speed of the animal when it left its footprints.

Extraordinary dinosaur tracks were found in Texas. Analysis showed that the tracks were made by adult and young saurischians. The adults must have walked 3.60 kilometers (2.2 miles) an hour and the young, 4 kilometers (2.5 miles) an hour. It was even possible to calculate that if these dinosaurs had moved at 20 kilometers (12.5 miles) an hour, the bones of their legs would have broken. (At the end of 1981, however, tracks of carnivorous bipeds that ran at 40 kilometers [25 miles] an hour were found.)

Terrible Lizards

When Richard Owen (1804–1892), the British anatomist and zoologist, began the study of enor-

An Eleven-Year-Old Paleontologist

In the nineteenth century, the carpenter Anning, who lived in the village of Lyme Regis in England, spent his leisure time looking for the numerous fossils that existed in that region. After his death, his daughter Mary continued to gather fossils in order to sell them to collectors. When she was 11 years old, she discovered the first almost complete fossil of an ichthyosaur. Later, she was the first to discover a pterodactyl in England.

mous reptile bones dug out in Europe, he understood that he was in the presence of fossils very different from those of known reptiles. They were so different that they must have belonged to a group of animals that became extinct a long time ago. He called them *dinosaurs* from the Greek meaning "terrible lizards."

Fishes: Living Fossils!

On December 22, 1938, a fishing boat captured a strange fish off the west coast of South Africa. A drawing of it was sent to L. B. Smith, an expert on fish. He declared that he could not have been more surprised if he had seen a dinosaur walk in the fields. This extraordinary fish was a coelacanth, representative of a group considered extinct since the end of the Cretaceous. Since then, some fifty of these fabulous fish have been caught; they are about 1.5 meters (5 feet) long and weigh some 70 kilograms (320 pounds).

Coelacanth

Dinosaur Discoverers

In a century and a half, paleontology has made tremendous discoveries. Here are the names (and for some paleontologists, their portraits) of those who contributed—and still contribute—to the progress of the knowledge of the past.

Nineteenth Century

Gideon Mantell (1790–1852)
In 1825 he described the first dinosaur teeth, which had been found by his wife, Mary Ann Mantell; they belonged to an *Iguanodon* of the Cretaceous of England.

Georges Cuvier (1769–1832)
Famous French anatomist

Gideon Mantell

and paleontologist, he identified as a "tooth of a rhinoceros" the first tooth of *Iguanodon* discovered by Mrs. Mantell. He acknowledged the error later, and together with Owen, he contributed to the description of dinosaurs.

Richard Owen (1804–1892)
Famous British anatomist and paleontologist, he created in 1842 the name *dinosaur.*

Sir Richard Owen

Thomas H. Huxley (1825–1895)
British anatomist, supporter of Charles Darwin, and grandfather of Aldous Huxley (author of *Brave New World*), he was the first to suggest that birds were related to dinosaurs.

Othniel C. Marsh (1831–1899)
American paleontologist, he discovered many fossil

Othniel C. Marsh

sites of dinosaurs in the central and western United States, in particular at Como Bluff (Wyoming) and the famous sites of the Cretaceous in Colorado.

Edward D. Cope
(1840–1897)
American paleontologist, he discovered several dinosaur fossil sites in the United States West. He competed with O. Marsh for the "conquest" of some dinosaur fossil sites at Como Bluff in 1879 and 1880.

Edward D. Cope

Friedrich von Huene

Early Twentieth Century

Friedrich von Huene
(1875–1965)
German paleontologist, he discovered and described Triassic dinosaurs in Germany *(Plateosaurus)*, as well as several fossil dinosaur sites in Argentina.

Franz Nopcsa (1875–1933)
Hungarian paleontologist, he found dinosaurs in Transylvania and contributed greatly to the classification of dinosaurs.

Henri F. Osborn
(1857–1935)
American paleontologist, he was famous for his investigation of elephants but also for his discovery and study of dinosaurs of the Morrison Formation (Wyoming) as well as the famous fossil dinosaur site at "Bone Cabin."

A. I. Efremov (1907–1972)
Soviet paleontologist, after

World War II he was in charge of Soviet expeditions to Mongolia, where he discovered large fossil dinosaur sites in the Gobi Desert, with abundant eggs of *Protoceratops*. He was also an author of science fiction (*Andromeda: A Space Age Tale*).

Modern Discoverers

Albert F. de Lapparant (1905–1975)
French paleontologist and geologist, he discovered a fossil dinosaur site in the Sahara Desert and searched for dinosaur tracks throughout the world (including Iran and Spitsbergen).

Edwin H. Colbert
American paleontologist, expert in Triassic dinosaurs, he discovered the first remains of dinosaurs in Antarctica and wrote several popular books on that subject, such as *Men and Dinosaurs,* which retraces the history of the discovery of the major dinosaur sites.

Philippe Taquet
French paleontologist, he studied dinosaur sites in Niger and Morocco and described the first remains discovered of dinosaurs in Thailand.

Alan Charig
British paleontologist, he is the author of numerous popular books on dinosaurs (*A New Look at Dinosaurs*).

José Bonaparte
Paleontologist, from Argentina, he studied the dinosaurs of Patagonia.

Tony Tulborn
Australian paleontologist, he studied dinosaur sites in Queensland (Australia) and is an expert in Triassic dinosaurs.

Zofice Kielan-Jaworowska
Polish paleontologist, she led the Polish-Mongolian paleontologic expeditions in the Gobi Desert and in western Mongolia (from 1963 to 1971), where numerous complete skeletons of ornithischian and saurischian dinosaurs from the Late Cretaceous were discovered.

Two Great American Museums

Two of the finest and most extensive collections of dinosaur fossils and reconstructions are at the American Museum of Natural History in New York and the Smithsonian Institution, Washington, D.C. The New York institution was incorporated in 1869 and sponsored many early expeditions, including those led by Roy Chapman Andrews. On display are reconstructions of a Brontosaurus *(67 feet long) and a* Tyrannosaurus *(47 feet long). There are also many models showing the natural habitats of the dinosaur.*

The National Museum of Natural History, a part of the Smithsonian, is located on the Mall in Washington in a building that was opened in 1910. Among the exhibits related to dinosaurs is the mounted skeleton of a Diplodocus *almost 80 feet long and 12 feet high. There are also reconstructions of a* Stegosaurus *and a* Pteranodon, *a flying reptile that lived in the dinosaur era.*

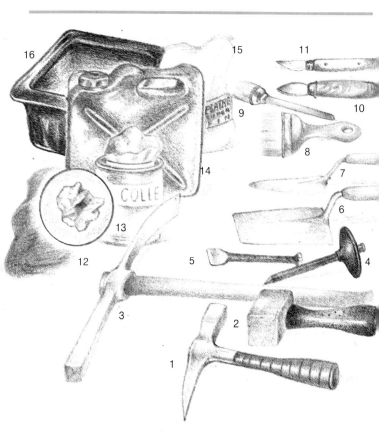

The tools of a paleontologist:

1. Geologic hammer

2. Sledgehammer

3. Pickax

4. Burin or chisel for hard rocks

5. Cold chisel

6 and 7. Trowels (to mix plaster or stir sand)

8 and 9. Brushes (to clean fossil bones)

10 and 11. Knives (to extract bones)

12 and 13. Crystals of glue to dissolve in alcohol

14. Water (to make plaster)

15. Bag of plaster of Paris

16. Plastic bowl (to mix plaster)

Stages of Research:

1. Paleontologists plan an expedition to search for fossils.

2. The fossil site: workers extract fossil bones.

3. In the laboratory, materials undergo final extraction.

4. Discoveries are examined under the microscope if fossils are small.

5. They are classified and analyzed.

6. The end results are publications and sometimes reconstruction of an animal.

Where Do Dinosaurs Come From?

It is known today that life on earth has constantly evolved, from the appearance of the first bacteria (the smallest and oldest living organism) to human beings.

Dinosaurs, as do all living beings, have a long history. They are reptiles that have amphibian ancestors, which in turn are descendants of fish.

How did the evolution from fish to dinosaurs occur? The three fundamental obstacles that had to be overcome were 1) the conquest of land by plants, 2) the breathing of air by animals, and 3) the possibility of these animals reproducing on land by means of special eggs that are different from those of amphibians.

What a strange sight our planet must have been during the Ordovician (second period of the Paleozoic, 440-500 million years ago)! The land-masses were entirely arid, only rocks, without plant or tree, except for some mosses and lichens.

During the Late Silurian, 400 million years ago, algae gradually evolved and climbed to the shores. They became terrestrial plants without roots and leaves and were only a few centimeters high. They were capable of standing erect, however, and had a vascular system that enabled them to bring water from the surface to the top of the plant. They are called *Psilopsida*. They soon developed, diversified, grew taller, and became increasingly complex. The appearance of plants on land was perhaps the most important step in the evolutionary process, because, as part of the process of

From amphibian to dinosaur: *The limbs of amphibians are at almost the same level as the body: the belly drags on the ground, and the legs do not lift them up (bottom).*
The limbs of reptiles allow them to lift themselves a little above the ground. In dinosaurs, the limbs were completely perpendicular to the ground. The belly did not touch the ground. Some of them, the bipeds, even lifted the forelegs completely.

photosynthesis, by which they nourished themselves, they transformed carbon dioxide into oxygen. Oxygen is indispensible for respiration in animals, including human beings.

Before the appearance of plants, the terrestrial atmosphere lacked oxygen.

45

It consisted mainly of methane, ammonia, hydrogen, and water vapor. Furthermore, lethal ultraviolet radiation produced by the sun surrounded the earth. Ultraviolet radiation transformed part of the oxygen produced by plants into ozone, thus forming a screen that radiation could not pass.

Owing to the action of plants, animals were eventually able to leave the water and spread over the continents. This was done first by crossopterygian fish.

At the end of the Devonian, two seasons followed each other: one was very dry and the other rainy. During the dry season, lakes and rivers dried up. Lacking water, fish barely survived. Some of them adapted to the new environment and tried to breathe air by developing a kind of lung. Leaning on their bony jaws, they succeeded in dragging themselves onto land, searching

During the Jurassic and the Cretaceous, dinosaurs conquered the earth:

1. Deinonychus
(dromeosaur of the Early Cretaceous)

2. Ornithomimus
(coelurosaur of the Late Cretaceous)

3. Coelurus
(coelurosaur of the Late Jurassic)

4. Stegosaurus
(stegosaur of the Late Jurassic)

5. Corythosaurus
(ornithopod of the Early Cretaceous)

6. Iguanodon
(ornithopod of the Early Cretaceous)

7. Triceratops
(ceratopsian of the Late Cretaceous)

8. Tyrannosaurus
(carnosaur of the Late Cretaceous)

9. Diplodocus
(sauropod of the Late Jurassic)

10. Brontosaurus
(sauropod of the Late Jurassic)

The Oldest Known Amphibian

The oldest known amphibian was Ichthyostega. *It lived at the end of the Devonian, about 340 million years ago. It was discovered by a Swedish paleontologist, Save Söderbergh, in Greenland. Measuring 1.20 meters (4 feet) in length, it had eardrums and strong limbs with toes. Because of its thorax consisting of numerous ribs, we know that it had lungs. Nevertheless, it must have lived mostly in water. There, it fed on its main food, fish, and it certainly returned there to lay eggs.*

Its skeleton preserved some similarities with that of fish, for instance its fin-shaped tail.

Its appearance marked the beginning of the conquest of land by vertebrates.

Ichthyostega

for water. These fish were the origin of amphibians. Amphibians are animals that reproduce and are born in water, live at first in the shape of a tadpole, then gradually change during growth and can eventually live on land. During the Devonian and the Carboniferous, 300 to 400 million years ago, the amphibians changed considerably.

The bones of the legs thickened in order to better support body weight. The muscles became stronger so that they could move without dragging themselves too much. The spine became sturdier. The eardrums evolved so that they could more easily detect sounds transmitted by air, which are weaker than those transmitted by water. They had eyelids to protect the eyes and tear glands to clean the eyes and keep them moist.

From Amphibian to Reptile

Amphibians conquered the land 350 million years ago. They breathed air and were able to spend most of their time out of the water. Nevertheless, they continued to return to water for food, to lay eggs, and to ensure the growth of their young.

Most amphibians disappeared at the end of the Permian, 225 million years ago. Their only descendants are newts and salamanders, ancestors of frogs and toads. The ancestor of the first reptile, however, was among the amphibians that dwelled on the earth during the Carboniferous.

There is no doubt that some amphibians became reptiles in the beginning of that period. They no longer needed water for food and reproduction. The answer was in the egg. It had a hard shell and contained everything so that the embryo (the future reptile) could develop and be born with the same shape and the same capacities as its parents, contrary to amphibians, which were born in the shape of tadpoles.

The Amniotic Egg

This egg is surrounded by a hard membrane that protects it from drying in the air. Inside, the embryo develops within a sac—the amnion—which contains a liquid, the amniotic liquid. The egg also contains two other sacs connected to the embryo. The first, the vitellus (the yolk sac), contains food for the development of the embryo. The other, the allantois, grows out of the digestive tract of the embryo and collects waste, in particular urine.

Fish and amphibians must lay a great number of eggs in order to secure their lineage. In water, these eggs are in fact at the mercy of numerouus predators: insects, crustaceans, and fish. Only about a hundred out of millions of eggs survive. Outside water, it is easier to hide eggs and less of them have to be laid. Reproduction therefore became easier for reptiles far away from water: large areas were open to them. The rapid spread of reptiles around the world occurred in the middle of the Carboniferous, over 300 million years ago.

Dinosaurs appeared during the Triassic, about 225 million years ago. They differed from other reptiles by the position of the limbs in relation to the body. They had legs placed straight beneath the body and thus were much farther off the ground than other reptiles. They reigned over the earth for almost 150 million years.

Indeed, during the

Cretaceous, everything seemed to the advantage of dinosaurs. They had conquered the earth and adapted to the requirements of climate, of the flora, and of the morphology of the continents. They seemed ready to live for another period as long as the one during which they had prospered. What could have abruptly stopped their advance?

Where Are Dinosaurs Displayed?

This selective, alphabetical, and international list gives some of the most important collections.

Australia
Australian Museum, Sydney
Queensland Museum, Brisbane

Canada
Museum of Natural Science, Ottawa (Ontario)
Provincial Park of Dinosaurs, Patricia (Alberta)

China
Museum of Natural History, Beijing (Peking)

France
Museum of Natural History, Aix-en-Provence
National Museum of Natural History, Paris

Germany
East: Museum of Natural History, East Berlin
West: Institute of Paleontology, Tübingen

Great Britain
British Museum, London
Pitt Rivers Museum, Oxford

Italy
Museum of Natural History, Venice

Niger
Museum of Natural History, Niamey

Poland
Academy of Sciences, Warsaw

Thailand
Museum of Mining and Geology, Bangkok

United States
Dinosaur National Monument, Jensen (Utah)
American Museum of Natural History, New York City
Smithsonian Institution, Washington, D.C.

USSR
Institute of Paleontology, Academy of Sciences, Moscow

Death of the Dinosaurs

Dinosaurs became extinct about 65 million years ago, during the Late Cretaceous, at the same time as numerous other animal species: marine and flying reptiles, marine invertebrates (ammonites, belemnites...).
Other similar events occurred earlier and happened again later. Very large groups of animals and plants have disappeared at various times during the history of our planet. These changes of fauna and flora have been used by scientists to date the succession of geologic periods.

Today, there are two major theories to explain the extinction of dinosaurs. Some geologists, paleontologists, and astronomers believe that it was a sudden event that lasted some tens of years because of a cosmic catastrophe, such as the impact of a large comet. Other paleontologists and biologists believe, on the contrary, that this extinction occurred gradually over 5 to 6 million years. Indeed, at the end of the Cretaceous, the sea regressed, exposing parts of continents. This was related to a cool-ing of the earth, which was critical enough so that dinosaurs, cold-blooded animals (as most scientists have long believed they were) became sluggish and gradually died.

A Killer Comet

Two American paleontologists, John Sepkoski and David Raup, used the computer to study the history of extinctions of species during the history of the earth: 250,000 species disappeared in 250 million years. These paleontologists con-

A killer comet: *Did a comet strike the earth's atmosphere, changing the amount of sunlight passing through, causing plants—and, eventually, dinosaurs—to die?*

firmed that mass extinctions occur every 26 million years. This regularity, they said, can be explained by a cyclic extraterrestrial event, such as the impact of a comet.

The basis of this assumption is the layer containing iridium deposited over the entire earth 65 million years ago. Iridium is a rare element found everywhere on the earth, but in very small quantities. Luis W. Alvarez, Walter Alvarez, and their coworkers at the University of California–Berkeley stated in several papers in 1979 and 1980 that a comet carrying this element fell on the earth at that time. A cloud of dust caused by the impact is supposed to have darkened the sky so that plants—which need light to live—disappeared rapidly. The food chain was thus interrupted and dinosaurs starved to death. Herbivores were the first to die, followed by carnivores. According to some astronomers, the fall of the comet is related to Nemesis, which is one of the names given to our sun's small companion star. The latter is assumed to complete its orbit in 26 million years and to cause

disturbances in the Oort cloud, a cloud of comets. Such disturbances may have caused some of these comets to hit the earth at each passage of Nemesis.

Other scientists believe that a mysterious planet, as yet unknown, the last planet of the solar system, may have had its orbit regularly modified by the influence of other planets. Every 28 million years, this mysterious planet is also supposed to cause disturbances in the Oort cloud. Finally, some scientists assume that when the solar system crosses the Milky Way, it may encounter interstellar clouds of dust that also disturb the Oort cloud.

From Crisis to Crisis

The above ways of explaining the extinction of dinosaurs seem somewhat far-fetched and are full of asssumptions. Furthermore, they do not explain why some species did not disappear together with dinosaurs.

Léonard Ginsburg, a paleontologist at the Natural Museum of Natural History at Paris, does not agree with these explanations. According to him, extinctions have not occurred every 26 or 28 million years.

Extinctions of species have occurred often, but all did not have the same importance:

— Some hundred minor crises have occurred during which a group disappeared from one region to go to another one.

— Some twenty major crises have existed during which entire groups disappeared.

There were two extremely important crises that took place. First, at the end of the Paleozoic, 230 million years ago, the reign of fish and amphibians diminished while reptiles began to take over. Second, between the Mesozoic and the Cenozoic, a group of reptiles (dinosaurs) died and left their place to mammals, which began their amazing development.

Evidence contrary to the catastrophe-iridium theory has also been found: in Montana, dinosaur fossils were discovered *above* the layer of iridium, and a thick layer of iridium (dating back 20 million years) was found without any associated disturbance among the fauna and flora.

A Planetary Event

Let us return to earth with more serious attempts to explain the event. It is necessary to find a hypothesis, an explanation that takes into account the entire problem, both on land and in the sea.

On land, all large reptiles (sauropods, carnosaurs, coelurosaurs, hadrosaurs, and ceratopsians), as well as flying reptiles, disappeared.

In the sea, marine reptiles (ichthyosaurs, plesiosaurs, and mosasaurs) died, as well as the two most important groups of invertebrates living in the seas during the Jurassic and the Cretaceous: ammonites and belemnites. Furthermore, most of the echinoderms, the brachiopods, and the mollusks became extinct. Such a catastrophe could have happened only because of an exceptionally important event on a planetary scale.

The Sea Retreated

It is known for sure that the sea retreated on a large scale at this time.

In the past, such retreats of the sea always caused great destruction of marine and terrestrial faunas.

Since the beginning of the Cambrian, 600 million years ago, the sea repeatedly invaded or retreated from continental margins, introducing each time a new fauna during its invasion and destroying it during its retreat.

It is known that marine life is more active and more abundant along the shores, on the continental shelf, in areas of shallow water where light and solar radiation favor the growth of algae, food for many animals.

The area of the continental shelf gently sloping from the shores to its edge, about 200 meters (650 feet) in depth, corresponds to that particular area of intense life (see map). Beyond the shelf, the slope increases rapidly and light no longer penetrates.

In the middle of the Cretaceous, the sea covered all of Europe up to the Urals. It even extended as far as

Europe in the middle of the Cretaceous:

Exposed lands

Continental shelf under shallow marine water

Deep seas.

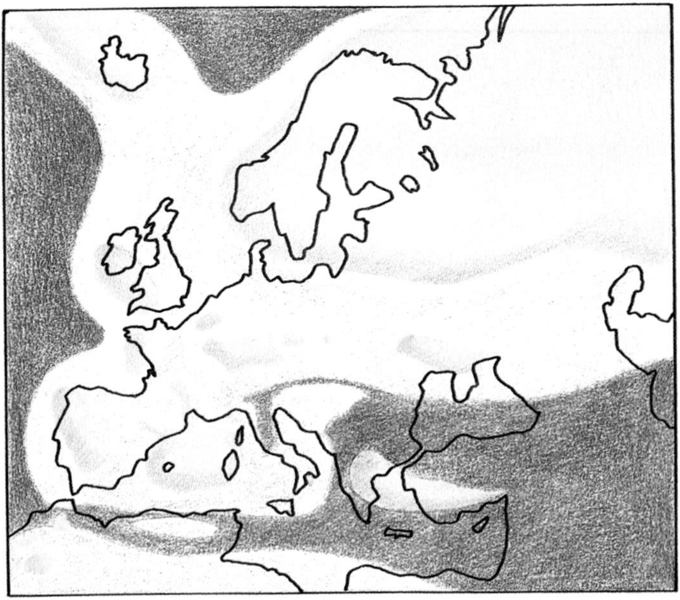

Africa in a wide marine seaway to join the Gulf of Guinea, thus dividing the African continent in two.

The Struggle for Life

At the end of the Cretaceous, the sea gradually retreated. It exposed Europe and the sea level was even further lowered. It would have been possible to walk 200 kilometers (125 miles) beyond the present-day port city of Brest before reaching the sea. Thus, the former shallow water continental shelf was reduced to a narrow fringe 5 to 10 kilometers (3 to 6 miles) wide.

Furthermore, it is believed today that the retreat of the sea was caused by the fact that a huge amount of seawater became locked as icecaps at the poles. The great retreats of marine shores were therefore related to glaciations.

The surface where marine organisms could live

Europe at the end of the Cretaceous: After the retreat of the sea, new lands became exposed at the expense of the continental shelf, formerly rich in fauna and flora.

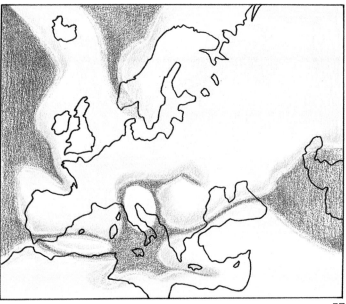

was thus reduced 100 to 300 times. Living space in the oceans was thus dramatically reduced. The struggle for life intensified. The numbers of individuals and species decreased greatly: the weakest and the least adaptable died.

Frozen To Death?

On the other hand, living space on land increased as much. However, the retreat of the sea modified climates, which became continental with harsh winters and warmer summers. When the sea spreads and invades the lands, climates are more moderate; when it retreats, the opposite occurs.

This difference of climate had catastrophic consequences for large reptiles. Today, the most important and most numerous reptiles live in the hot areas on earth. In temperate regions, they are rare and of a small size. Going towards the poles, they become increasingly rare because these cold-blooded animals with variable temperature depend upon that of the environment and cannot stand the cold.

At the end of the Cretace-

Hypothetical battle between a plesiosaur (right) and a mosasaur, a giant marine lizard (left).

ous, when the climate became continental after the retreat of the sea, dinosaurs and other reptiles could not bear cold winters; they were not sufficiently warm to maintain their activity. Therefore, they became increasingly sluggish and died slowly but surely because they could neither dig lairs nor protect themselves from their enemies in other ways. Only smaller reptiles survived. However, warm-blooded vertebrates—birds and mammals—adapted to the climate and reached their well-known development.

Thus, 65 million years ago, the most extraordinary animals ever known on earth disappeared. They were so fabulous that ever since their past existence was discovered, people have been unable to stop dreaming about them and imagining their ways of living, raising questions about the causes of their death, and often inventing, in no scientific fashion, events that might have caused their extinction. Even trying to revive them, some people were persuaded that they had "seen" the Loch Ness monster, a survivor of a legendary past.

Fauna before the marine regression: *During the Jurassic and the Cretaceous, the sea covered a large portion of the continental shelf. There, a gentle slope descended gradually, and a shallow sea covered it. Solar rays penetrated the water easily and allowed the flora to live and proliferate, thus providing abundant food to marine animals.*
The influence of the sea led to a warm and humid climate perfectly suited for dinosaurs and other reptiles that could not survive in harsher climates.

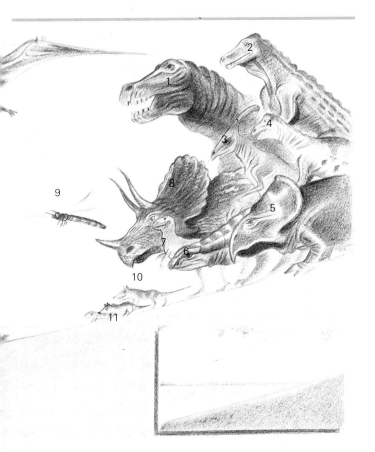

1. Tyrannosaurus
2. Iguanodon
3. Parasaurolophus
4. Coerulosaurus
5. Protoceratops
6. Ankylosaurus
7. Peinonychilde
8. Triceratops
9. Dragonfly
10. Alphadon

11. Triconodon
12. Pteranodon
13. Plesiosaurus
14. Ichthyosaurus
15. Sea lily
16. Sea urchin
17. Ammonites
18. Belemnites
19 and 20. Rudists

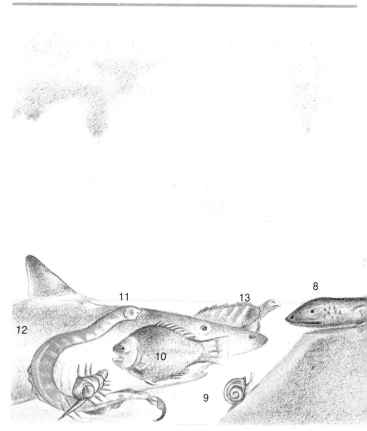

Fauna after marine regression: *It is known that at the end of the Cretaceous, glacial caps expanded at the poles, which caused a lowering of the sea level and cooling of the climate.*

<u>*Decrease of sea level:*</u> *The continental shelf previously covered with water sheltered a very rich marine life. When the sea retreated, this shelf was reduced to a narrow band where fauna and flora could not subsist. Immediately beyond the shelf edge, the depth of the sea increased rapidly. The two most abundant groups of invertebrates, ammonites and belemnites, as well as marine reptiles, disappeared.*

<u>*Colder Climate:*</u> *Dinosaurs and other terrestrial reptiles could not resist this cold wave. Only a few survived, such as crocodiles, snakes, and turtles. Strange birds appeared, which could not fly but ran, whereas mammals, capable of protecting themselves from the cold, gradually took the place of dinosaurs.*

1. Bird

2. Gastornis (Europe): These wingless running birds lived at the beginning of the Tertiary in empty lands left by the extinct dinosaurs

3. Snake

4. Marsupial (Triconodon)

5. Marsupial (Deltatheridium)

6. Crocodile

7. Dragonfly

8. Amphibian

9. Gastropod

10. Fish

11. Lamprey

12. Shark

13. Turtle

14. Diatryma (North America)

Reptiles, Ancestors of Birds

At the beginning of the Mesozoic, small reptiles living in trees began to develop membranes connected to their ribs. They did not really fly but glided when falling from trees.

At the beginning of the Jurassic, pterosaurs appeared. They somewhat resembled present bats with a membrane linking together their forelimbs and hindlimbs. The most famous flying reptiles are Pterodactylus *and* Pteranodon. *The wingspan of the latter could reach 15 meters (50 feet). Their hollow bones made them very light. They had an elongated skull, and the jaw of* Pterodactylus *was armed with teeth.*

The true ancestors of birds were certainly small biped dinosaurs, not yet discovered. The first bird was Archaeopteryx *(Jurassic), whose body was covered with feathers. It retained, however, some characteristics of reptiles, such as its two clawed fingers on the forelimbs, its long tail, and its teeth.*

Archaeopteryx

Reptiles, Ancestors of Mammals

At the beginning of the Permian, 280 million years ago, the earth was ruled by mammallike reptiles. The oldest were pelycosaurs, rather clumsy creatures. Amidst them were the ancestors of mammals.

Some mammallike reptiles adopted new ways of living: although the others were carnivores, they started to graze plants.

At the end of the Permian, another group of mammallike reptiles appeared: cynodonts. They were found in Africa, South America, China, and in the Soviet Union. Nimble and slender, they were as tall as a cat or a wolf and had the teeth of a shrew, and the body was apparently covered by hair. This hair was not as yet very insulating, but later it helped to protect mammals against the cold.

At the end of the Triassic, all mammallike reptiles disappeared. They evolved into mammals, which were able to develop only when dinosaurs had disappeared.

Cynodont

Dinosaur Tales

Every civilization on earth had fabulous tales that were deeply rooted in the imagination of human beings. They told about the existence of strange, enormous, and often dangerous and aggressive monsters. In many countries, they were fire-spitting dragons, sometimes powers of darkness and evil, often guardians of hidden treasures.

Today, everybody knows that dragons never existed and that dinosaurs have disappeared. The discovery of bones of these huge, strange, and fabulous beasts has revived the imagination of men. These animals became the source of marvellous tales of their existence among us and of the way they disappeared.

Sheer Dreams

The Loch Ness Monster
This is certainly the most famous among the inventive stories of dinosaurs still living today.

Loch Ness is a lake in Scotland. In 1934, a surgeon from London took a photograph of a strange being that very much resembled a plesiosaur with a long neck. However, the photograph is very hazy; one does not know whether it was taken close up or from far away. The zoologist Burton attested that instead of a dinosaur, it was, in fact, a sea otter diving into water.

In 1975, Robert Scott and Peter Rhins showed other photographs of the monster in the lake. This time, one can imagine a body, a triangular fin, and a grotesque head. According to them, the animal must be a reptile with a long neck and fins. Upon careful examination of the pictures, however, one can see that it might just as well be the wreck of

A "photo of the Loch Ness Monster": *Reported sightings of this creature have stirred imaginations over the years.*

a Viking ship. The body would be the hull; the fin, the rudder; and the head, the bow of the ship.

These photographs were nothing more than a hoax.

Plesiosaurs lived in warm waters: Loch Ness is a very cold lake.

Plesiosaurs lived 80 million years ago: Loch Ness is only 12,000 years old.

The "Raou" of New Guinea

New Guinea is one of the largest islands in the Pacific Ocean located just north of Australia. It is a very wild area, which was little explored until the fifties.

Some 40 years ago, a young Dutch couple, Mr. and Mrs. Miller, decided to go to New Guinea for their honeymoon. It was an unforgettable trip.

While visiting the country, the Millers met an unknown tribe, the Kirrirri. These people frequently used a tool resembling the point of an elephant tusk or the horn of a rhinoceros. The Millers asked the people of the villages where they acquired this "horn."

The New Guineans drew in the sand a kind of lizard with a long neck, an enormous arched body, and a long tail. Its head was adorned by a bony shield and its back had projecting triangular scales.

The animal was supposed to be some 12 meters (20 feet) long. Of course, the Millers asked to see it. After a journey of several hours, they arrived on a plateau that dominated an immense swamp. They hid and waited.

Suddenly, the beast emerged from the reeds. According to Miller: "As if obeying our desire, this colossal survivor of the age of dinosaurs trampled across the swamp. At one time it lashed its tail against some grasses so far away from its head that I believed that the tail belonged to another beast. For a split second I saw its horned end.

"I heard the hissing of the beast: Raou-ou...Raou-ou..."

Miller released the shutter of his camera. The monster stopped, stood on its hindlegs, and threw its snakelike neck in his direction.

In the book he wrote to narrate their adventure, Miller described the monster in the following terms: "It was covered with irregular scales which were arranged like armor as if they were meant for camouflage."

Unfortunately, Miller's photographs are nowhere to be found. Furthermore, nobody saw them. He did not bring back any "horns," which, according to him, the natives owned in great number.

Furthermore, his "dinosaur" resembles rather a mixture of several species of dinosaurs that lived during different epochs. Indeed, his dinosaur had the bony shield of a *Triceratops*, the long neck and tail of a *Brontosaurus* or *Diplodocus*, and the body of a *Stegosaurus*.

It is true that zoologists and paleontologists have not yet discovered all species of dinosaurs—but what a farce, to mix so many known characteristics of other dinosaurs! It is hardly conceivable that nature would be able to produce such a mixture of so many dissimilar parts. However, nothing could be easier for the human imagination.

Mokélé Mbêmbé of the Congo

Whereas the Loch Ness monster and the Raou were certainly born from the imagination of some individuals badly in need of thrills, Mokélé Mbêmbé seems to be a legend known by the populations of the lower Congo Basin.

At the beginning of the century when this legend was first told to Europeans, the Congo Basin, with its vast flooded areas, its deep forests, and its swamps was not well-known and lent itself well to the creation of a mysterious tale. The subject of this tale is Mokélé Mbêmbé, an animal larger than a hippopotamus, which has a long neck, a head with a horn, a very long tail, and is completely covered by a smooth gray-brown hide.

This animal was supposed to live in caves dug in argillaceous banks beneath water and to eat vines with white flowers. It is supposed not to kill humans in order to eat them, because it is vegetarian, but to protect itself.

This tale comes from regions that are very far apart yet always located in the Congo Basin.

No scientific proof about the existence of this animal was given. Some hazy photographs seem to show a large-sized turtle. Africans themselves call it a legend. None of them ever saw the animal. It is simply a story that is repeated from generation to generation, similar to tales of dragons that fed —sometimes still feed—our Western stories.

Sheer Jokes

Ever since they were discovered, dinosaurs have haunted the human imagination, even to a point that in order to explain their extinction, we invented all kinds of possible and imaginable reasons without seeing that they were quite unlikely.

Philippe Taquet, Director of the National Museum of Natural History at Paris, counted eighty-one such inventions. Below are the funniest or the most widespread ones.

Noah's Ark: It was said that Noah, inviting a pair of each animal species on board his ark, forgot dinosaurs.

Death by old age: After having lived on earth for 150 million years, dinosaurs are supposed to have all died of senility.

Death by stupidity: Having such a minute brain compared with their huge size, dinosaurs might have died because of excessive stupidity.

Victims of depression or stress: Dinosaurs are believed to have become depressive, melancholic, and suicidal. According to another hypothesis, they all died of strokes.

Starved to death: Some caterpillars are assumed to have devoured all the vegetal food of vegetarian dinosaurs. Thus, they starved to death and were soon followed by carnivorous dinosaurs, no longer able to feed on herbivorous dinosaurs.

Poison: Another explanation is that herbivorous dinosaurs may have eaten toxic plants, which poisoned them.

Death by aggression: Two hypotheses were consid-

ered. One: Carnivorous dinosaurs became too numerous; they killed all herbivorous dinosaurs and finally themselves. Two: Small mammals proliferated and preyed on all nests of dinosaurs, thus preventing new generations from being born.

Death by epidemics: One or more deadly diseases may have killed the dinosaurs.

Victims of droughts: The climate may have become too hot. Plants disappeared and with them all food for herbivorous dinosaurs.

Frozen to death: Volcanoes are assumed to have spewed out great amounts of ash that formed a screen against solar radiation necessary for the growth of plants. The latter disappeared and dinosaurs also.

A dinosaur dies *because of its weight. This is yet another crazy explanation of the death of dinosaurs. They are supposed to have been victims of their huge mass.*

A Triceratops eats toxic plants! *The imagination of people who searched for causes for the extinction of dinosaurs is fertile!*

These "theories" on the death of dinosaurs are all imaginary; they were thought of mostly by individuals who were not paleontologists.

They all forgot one extremely important fact: dinosaurs did not die alone. Numerous other animals died also: pterosaurs, ichthyosaurs, mosasaurs, sarcopterygians, ammonites, belemnites, rudists, and others. It is hard to believe that all these animals disappeared at the same time, each one for another reason. We must admit that they all died at the same time and because of the same cause: marine regression during the Cretaceous.

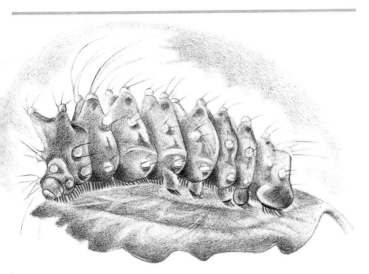

A caterpillar, killer of dinosaurs... *Caterpillars are believed to have eaten the leaves on which herbivorous dinosaurs fed. Thus the latter died and were followed by carnivorous dinosaurs, for which the herbivores had been the primary source of food.*

A small mammal. *This might have been the cause of the extinction of dinosaurs. These small animals are supposed to have eaten all dinosaur eggs.*

Glossary

Amber: Fossil resin of some conifers. Insects become glued to resin oozing out from trees. Thereafter, these insects become fossilized, being protected by the resin. The exterior of the body remains intact but the internal organs disappear.

Ammonites: The most important cephalopods of the Mesozoic.

Ankylosaurs: Dinosaurs of the Late Cretaceous.

Belemnites: Suborder of fossil dibranchiate cephalopod mollusks. Most probably ancestors of the living cuttlefish.

Carnivores: Meat-eating animals.

Carnosaurs: Saurischian dinosaurs, the ruling predators. The best known is *Tyrannosaurus*. In spite of their large size, they apparently ran fast (footprints discovered in North America show that their strides were longer than 3.5 meters [11.5 feet]). They were carnivores and fed mostly on decaying carcasses.

Ceratopsians: Dinosaurs of the Late Cretaceous with a horn on the head and a bony shield at the back of the neck.

Class: Major division in animals and plants. A class includes several orders and suborders. Thus, *Diplodocus* belongs to the suborder of sauropods, to the order of saurischians, and to the class of reptiles.

Coelurosaurs: Important group of dinosaurs. All are saurischians and bipeds. Many were carnivores; some specialized in the looting of nests.

Comets: Heavenly bodies that gravitate around the sun in elliptical orbits. Originating certainly from a cloud of heavenly bodies in orbit around the solar system, the Oort cloud, comets consist of frozen gases and dust. When they pass close to the sun, some portions disintegrate because of the heat: this is the tail of a comet.

Dinosaurs: Important group of archosaurian reptiles that are divided into two orders: ornithischians and saurischians. The name means "terrible lizard."

Family: Subdivision of the classification of animals and plants. A family consists of a certain number of genera, and several families form an order.

Fossilization: Preservation in layers of rocks of remains or traces of activity belonging to past living organisms.

Genus: Subdivision of classification that includes related species.

Gondwana: Former continent in the southern hemisphere including what is known today as South America, Africa, India, Australia, and Antarctica.

Herbivores: Plant-eating animals.

Ichthyosaurs: The most specialized marine reptiles. They lived during the entire Mesozoic, in particular the Jurassic.

Laurasia: Former continent in the northern hemisphere including present-day North America, Europe, and Asia.

Mesosaurs: Anapsid reptiles that adapted to aquatic life at the end of the Carboniferous.

Mesozoic: Includes three periods: Triassic, Jurassic, and Cretaceous. It began 225 million years ago and ended 65 million years ago.

Order: See Class and Family.

Oort Cloud: See Comets.

Ornithischians: Dinosaurs with a birdlike pelvis.

Paleontologists: Scientists who study fossils.

Pangaea: Early supercontinent that included Gondwana, Laurasia, and all other continents.

Period: Subdivision of geologic eras. Each period is characterized by specific plant and animal fossils.

Permian: Last period of the Paleozoic Era. It started about 280 million years ago and ended 225 million years ago.

Plesiosaurs: Marine reptiles living during the Triassic.

Predator: Any animal that hunts and kills other animals for food.

Pterosaurs: Flying reptiles that appeared at the beginning of the Jurassic.

Reptiles: A class of terrestrial vertebrates with scaly skin. They laid eggs in which the embryo developed in an amniotic sac, similarly to birds and mammals.

Saurischians: Dinosaurs with a lizardlike pelvis.

Sauropods: Group of saurischian dinosaurs that were abundant during the Jurassic and the Cretaceous (*Brachiosaurus* and *Diplodocus*).

Suborder: See Class.

Species: A group of animals or plants that are characterized by the hereditary transmission of a specific group of genes. Members of the same species reproduce among themselves but not with members of other species.

Thecodonts: Primitive archosaurian reptiles, believed to be the ancestors of dinosaurs. They lived from the Late Permian to the Late Triassic.

Index

References to illustrations are in italics.

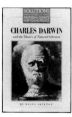

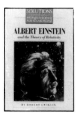